I MISS TALKING
TO YOU

CONSTANCE LONGMIRE

I Miss Talking to You

Copyright 2013

Constance Longmire

All rights reserved.

ISBN: 978-1-938950-29-2

Printed in USA by Greater Is He Publishing
9824 E. Washington St. Chagrin Falls, Ohio 44023

P.O. Box 46115 Bedford, Ohio 44146

http://www.greaterishepublishing.com

Office: 216.288.9315

DEDICATION

To Mama and Daddy: I Miss Talking to you.

I thank my God for every remembrance of you.

Phil. 1:3

CONTENTS

	Acknowledgments	vii
	Foreword	viii
Chapter 1	My Beautiful Mother was Diagnosed With Dementia	1
Chapter 2	Being Born With a Veil	7
Chapter 3	Mama, Debbie Won't Let Me Follow Her	10
Chapter 4	Connie, You're the Lead Off	14
Chapter 5	My Parents Spoke In a Strange Language	18
Chapter 6	Be Quiet, Please!	20
Chapter 7	Mr. Harvey Peek	23
Chapter 8	Mama Sees Angels	27
Chapter 9	Bye, Mama, I'm Gonna Run Away	29
Chapter 10	Think Yourself Happy	32
Chapter 11	Daddy to the Rescue	38

Chapter 12	Mama Cooks an Apple Pie	44
Chapter 13	Mama Goes to the Assisted Living Facility	47
Chapter 14	Mom Goes to Heaven	55
Chapter 15	Homegoing Celebration "I Leave You Praise"	59
Chapter 16	Christmastime at the Peek's Home	62
Chapter 17	We Are Family	67
Chapter 18	Conclusion of the Matter	70
	About the Author	77

ACKNOWLEDGMENTS

I would like to thank my Lord and Savior Jesus Christ, Who comforted me, and continues to comfort me with his love! "Even as it is meet for me to think this of you all, I have you in my heart…" Phil. 1:7

Ken, Matt & Kay

The Honorable Bishop Norman L. & Dr. Rita Helen Wagner

Bishop C. Shawn (Pastor)

and First Lady Evangelist Krista Tyson

Evangelist Sherri Brogdon

Dr. Gloria Foward

Dr. Valarie Cooper

A very special thank you to my mom's friends at Mt. Calvary Pentecostal Church: Mother Green, Mother Joseph, and Mother Levels.

Foreword

Alzheimer's, the most common form of dementia, is a disease that attacks the brain. It can have a severe interference with one's cognitive function and daily living. Symptoms slowly develop and gradually worsen over time eventually causing problems with daily tasks such as carrying on a conversation and properly responding to one's surroundings. According to the Alzheimer's Association 2013, this disease affects over 5 million Americans and it is the sixth leading cause of death in the United States. The age of onset is typically 65 years of age and older but an early onset can start between 40 and 50 years of age. Risk factors include age, family history of the disease and heredity.

Caring for an individual with Alzheimer's disease can be frustrating, challenging and also rewarding. Alzheimer's impacts the caregiver's daily life; mentally, physically and emotionally. As Alzheimer's patients lose their abilities, the caregiver can experience overwhelming emotions, fatigue, exhaustion, isolation, loneliness and challenged resources as the demand increases for care and independence decreases for the loved one. This can also be a rewarding experience for the caregiver as bonds deepen through care and companionship. Through this experience relationships can grow and new ones can form through support and education.

In Dr. Longmire's book, *I Miss Talking to You,* the reader is permitted to experience the struggles and rewards of being a caregiver and a daughter to her mother as she battles Alzheimer's disease. Dr. Longmire's courageous spirit, compassion and determination to be there for her mother during the pleasant and not so pleasant times as the disease progressed brings awareness to society about firsthand experience with such a debilitating disease. To witness one's own loved one's mental and physical capacities decline and knowing that there is no cure only medication to minimize/mask the symptoms is very heart wrenching. Dr. Longmire is a very strong woman; her and her siblings' commitment to caring for their mother with Alzheimer's is an extraordinary gift, and wanting to help spread awareness of Alzheimer's disease is commendable.

Ileta E. Randall, RN

CHAPTER 1

My Beautiful Mother Was Diagnosed With Dementia

I remember it like it was yesterday, that day the doctor told me that my mom had dementia. "How could that be?" or "How could this have happened?" I kept asking myself. My mom has always been a very friendly, happy, active person. She did not smoke or drink alcohol, but still, she was stricken with this disease.

I kept asking myself several questions:

- How could this happen to such a good, Godly person?
- Why did God allow this to happen?
- What will people who know her think when she does not recognize them?
- What will people say about her?
- How do I deal with this diagnosis?
- Who can I talk to about my fear of losing Mom, as I know her?
- Who will she become? Will she still remember me?
- She's a minister of the Gospel. Will she forget the Word that she knows so well?

***

My mom was a beautiful Christian lady. She was "saved," baptized in Jesus' name and filled with the Holy Ghost. She loved the Lord with all of her might. We were raised in a Christian home with Christian values. My mom prayed and sang songs about the Lord. She believed in modest apparel and wore long skirts and dresses. She always smelled of perfume and powder. She never wanted to smell, and she would tell me, "Connie, don't let me stink. If I get to where I can't smell myself, clean me up and don't let me stink." I promised her that I would fulfill her instruction, and by the grace of God, I tried to keep my word from that day on.

She was very supportive of my endeavors. When I began my career as a motivational and conference speaker, she said to me, "I don't know what that is but you will be good at it." She often told me that I was the 'lead off,' in her words meaning I was a leader.

I hated when she told me that because it made me feel insecure about what I was going to do. "Connie, you the lead off. Someone has to do it," she said, and I successfully met each goal. I remember her teaching me about the Bible when I was young. She was never too much of a TV watcher, but she read a lot. In her later years, she watched the news and the judge shows. She loved to garden and had the prettiest flowers on the street. She also planted vegetables, such as corn, tomatoes, scallions, and greens. One year she planted pumpkin seeds and gave my daughter the first pumpkin that came from her garden. We put it on our porch, and it looked like it came from a store instead of her yard.

In November 2010, I was awakened by a phone call from a family member telling me that Mama was stomach-sick and wanted to go to the hospital. I took her, and the doctors found a minor condition in her stomach. They referred to her age, and asked for my consent to do a CAT scan. I consented and the doctor told me she had dementia. I must admit I felt like a piece of me melted away. It wasn't about her anymore, but about me. "How can I live without my mother?" I did not at first believe the diagnosis of the doctor. She was alert, talking and acting like my mom.

I cried for several days, asking myself questions over and over again. It felt like I had been pushed off a cliff, falling with nothing to hold on to. I needed to get a grip on something so I would not hit rock bottom. As I look back now, I realize God was carrying me in His loving arms. He held me so I didn't hit rock bottom.

This was the beginning of a new journey for me.

How did you feel when your loved one was diagnosed with an illness?

Note from Dr. Constance:

It is very important that you continue with the positives in life. Reach out to friends and get counseling, talk about how your feelings to a trusted confidant.

_____
_____
_____
_____
_____
_____
_____
_____
_____
_____
_____
_____
_____
_____
_____
_____
_____

I Miss Talking to You

CHAPTER 2

Being Born With A Veil

I am one of twelve children and eleventh in the Peek pecking order. Although there were a dozen of us, I never felt neglected. I have to be honest: I was very much loved, not spoiled, but much loved. My mom was a very caring woman who loved her children and husband very much. Although twelve kids may not have been in their plans, I never thought they regretted having any of us.

My mother shared the story of my birth with me many times while I was growing up. I remember wondering why she was telling me that and what I would gain from it. I was amazed that Mama remembered every step of my birth, and somehow that meant I stood out from the others. That made me feel very special, but she might have been using my birth as a guilt mechanism to keep me in line.

Ok, now to my birth as my mother told it to me. On a very calm and cool October day, my mom unexpectedly went into labor. She was taken to the hospital in the next town, and our family physician was called. In my small town, the local doctor was not only the pediatrician, but also the 'medical doctor' indeed. He handled all kinds of bumps, breaks, ailments, sickness, baby deliveries, and so on. I remember he was an older, heavyset gentleman with white hair and a voice that was barely above a whisper. He also made house calls and came to our home on occasions when we were sick. He carried a black doctor's bag with him and I thought it was very curious he did not have any candy or gum like our laundry man. All he had were tonic and elixirs.

My mom expected to give birth to me soon after she arrived at the hospital, but she did not. Her doctor entered the room, dressed in white, and nurses were all around him. He told my mom to push and she tried several times, but I did not arrive. When labor started, she moaned and groaned, for the pains were excruciating. She told me the pain was so bad that she asked God to take her life (I am so glad He did not). Her water had broken, but I still wasn't born. At this point in her story I asked, "Why didn't he just give you a caesarian?" and she said the doctor did not believe in them. After many long hours of pushing and moaning, she gave birth to me naturally and without medication. I came forth all red and with a white sack all over my body. My mother heard one of the nurses say loudly, "She's born with the veil on her." After staying in the hospital for a week, my mom was sent home. Although I was covered with what they called a "veil," medical doctors today would explain that my mom had a dry birth and what covered my body was the placenta.

My aunt came to visit us and they put petroleum jelly on my skin to remove the veil. I turned red as they gently rubbed it on my skin and peeled it off. Mama told me that it was in my hair, on my face, and all over my skin. After she told me this story, I just stared at her in amazement, and then went on my way.

According to the old saying, if you are born with a veil, you have a sixth sense. I don't know whether or not I do, but I can say for sure I am blessed and highly favored.

I would love to hear my mother tell me this story again. I would listen more attentively and deliberately. I would ask more questions about my birth.

As I now replay this story in my mind, I say to myself, "Mama, I miss talking to you."

CHAPTER 3

Mama, Debbie Won't Let Me Follow Her

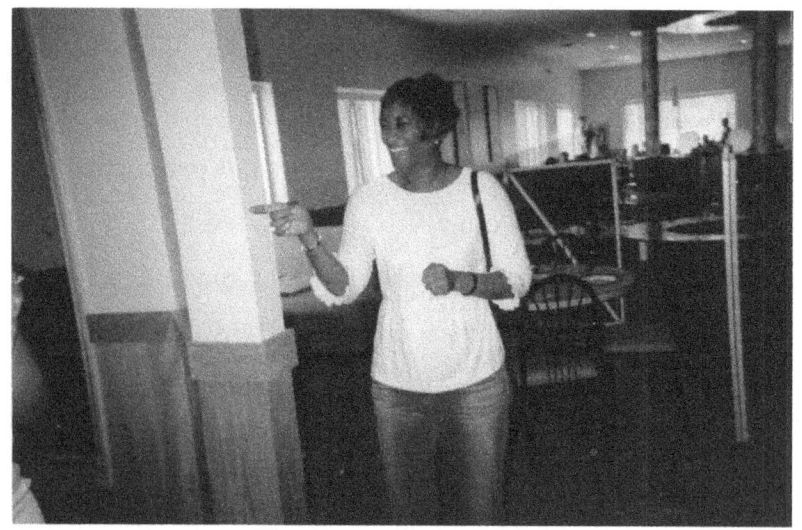

That's my sister, Debbie

We had a lot of land in the rural area where I grew up. We had three separate gardens. In our yard were cedar trees and a garden of sunflowers. When I wasn't working in the garden, I was pretending to be a Hollywood actress and Broadway dancer. I sang and danced. When my mom wasn't around, I sang along with the radio. In my early teens, I became more interested in my sister's activities, and wanted to spend more time with her.

My sister Debbie was, and still is, a very gregarious and outgoing person, living her life to the fullest degree. Whenever she is around, the room is filled with laughter and fun. Being the closest sister to me in age, I wanted to hang with her. I admired her zest for life. She had lots of friends and the guys went crazy over her. One day when I thought I was old enough to go out with her and she said "no," I went running to Mama and Dad. I complained, "Debbie won't let me go with her." They made her take me with her. In her defense, I admit that I could be a brat and whiny at times. While in the car with her, there was total silence, but I didn't care. I was hanging with my cool sister Debbie. I liked to follow her to see her in action. She made friends easily, and she didn't worry about anything. After hearing what she and her friends were talking about, I wanted to leave and go back to my world of singing and dancing. Their discussion was too complicated to interest me.

I watched Debbie like a cat staring at its prey, wanting to mimic her actions. She would do cartwheels up and down our driveway, and she was great in track and field. I would try to do a cartwheel and run track—don't even think about it. I lacked coordination and motivation, so while she did cartwheels and ran, I sat on the steps and sang.

One of my fondest childhood memories of Debbie was her pair of blue jeans that had a butterfly patch on the back right side. I coveted those jeans and wanted to wear them sooooo badly. When she wore them she got the attention of the guys. The butterfly patch had multiple colors in it and she picked out a color-coordinated shirt. She was such a fashionista! I asked her to let me wear them, but she didn't. Well, the day finally came that she no longer wanted them. *Hallelujah!* She was throwing out a bag of clothes and in that bag were those jeans. I picked them up, Mama washed them, and I wore them to school. I thought I was "hot stuff." I would twist and smile, wave and speak to everyone, imitating Debbie with charisma and confidence.

I was Debbie for a day, laughing, cool, and confident. Someone at school noticed that those were Debbie's jeans and they asked about her. WELL, I quickly snapped out of it. After a day of being and acting like Debbie, I came home exhausted. When I shared that part of my day with Mama, she told me to be who I am, and when I was grown, I could be whatever I wanted. She gave me a life lesson of being "Connie Peek," not "Debbie Peek."

I can almost hear mama now, lovingly chastising me for trying to grow up too fast. Although it was exhausting being Debbie for a day, it was still fun.

This was the first lesson I remember of Mama teaching me to be who I am and not to compare myself with others.

This was printed and written by permission of Debbie, whom I still admire and follow.

CHAPTER 4

Connie, You're the Lead Off

Boy, did I hate it when Mama said that to me. In her way, using her vocabulary, she was telling me that I was a leader and a pioneer in many things.

Growing up, Mama would tell me, "There's something about you, Connie, you know that you were born with that veil, you're the lead off!" Telling that to me as a child, I thought, *there goes another one of those southern terms that I don't understand.* I was a laidback child with a great imagination. I was observant and listened to conversations around me. I always wanted to be aware of my surroundings, and I hated surprises. I was, and still am very creative, and ideas come to my mind fast and furiously. Some ideas I act on and some I do not.

I remember when I started my public speaking and conference-hosting endeavors. Mama would say enthusiastically, "Go on–you can do it." When I talked to her about my 'Life Coaching' business, she said, "I don't know what that is, but if you like to do it, then do it, Connie."

I would tell Mama my ideas, and what I wanted to do in life. She said, "Connie, you have to be the lead off or the leader in what you want to do." Many times the ideas would scare me. They seemed bigger than I and required more money than I had, but I kept pushing. I asked her why God made me like this. She reminded me that I had a purpose in life and in due time God would reveal it to me. I later came to realize this is just the way God wired me. I must say I do have my fearful times, my uneasy times, and times where I am staring life in the face and thinking *"What now?"* But I remember the word 'purpose' and know God will reveal it to me.

Many times now I long for her loving interpretation of what is going on in my life. But I remind myself of her words about God having a purpose for me. If I had five more minutes with her, I would tell her again that she was right.

I am a professor at a renowned research university, a diversity representative, and the recipient of the Kent State University President's Award. This is awarded to people who are stellar in their field. I graduated from the Institute for Excellence for Outstanding Leaders. I'm responsible for my team receiving the Diversity Trail Blazer Award. I've received more awards and many accolades. I've had the privilege of speaking at conferences, churches, businesses and non-profit organizations.

My presentations on Diversity Encounters, Loving the Skin You're In, and The Art of Communication have received many stellar reviews. I am also a minister of the Gospel of Christ. After hearing one of my presentations, an organization made an offer for the rights to publish my life story (I told them No). I humbly list these accomplishments, noting that all the glory goes to GOD!!

You see, my mom was right. My life has a purpose and I am destined for greatness. Yes, I had to take the lead, the hits, and the criticisms for many things, but I do not mind. Mama helped prepare me for my purpose.

I'm sure she is looking down from Heaven in the midst of a cloud of witnesses, cheering me on saying, "Connie, you have to be the lead off—go on, you can do it!"

CHAPTER 5

My Parents Spoke in a Strange Language

My parents were from Crawfordsville, Georgia. Moving to the North, as they called it, was good for them. The Jim Crow Laws, prejudice, and bigotry were so strong in the South that they came to Ohio for better opportunities and a better quality of life. Moving north, they brought their southern dialect, which included metaphors and similes.

The following are examples of some of the expressions my parents used when I was growing up: (The bulleted line is what my parents said; the interpretation is in italics)

- Give you what Patty gave the drum.
  I will spank you.
- What ail you chowl
  What's the matter with you, child?
- John Brown the luck.
  Not sure, but used as 'dog-gone-it.'

- I will pay you for the old and the new.
  You will be disciplined for what you did in the past that I did not punish you for and what you did recently.
- Dry it up.
  Stop crying.
- Poe (poor) as Job's turkey.
  Used to describe someone who is having a hard time financially.
- Sat a pun.
  Rear end.
- Settle the score.
  Get a good understanding in a disagreement.
- Can't a dog wag his tail?
  This is the truth and it cannot be disputed.
- God Scandalous.
  Very awful or very disturbing.
- I ain't stu'in you.
  I am not studying you.

I could go on about these things. To this day, from time to time, my siblings and I will still use these terms when we talk to each other.

CHAPTER 6

Be Quiet, PLEASE!

My father was a very hard worker and entrepreneur. We owned an asphalt company called *Peek Asphalt*. My dad owned a yellow dump truck and employed a staff of about six guys. His business was quite lucrative. I often admired how he worked for six months a year, and then in the winter and early spring, he used his truck to haul things. I wanted him to show me how his business worked but he would not. He believed that girls should learn to cook and clean, and boys should be business-minded.

My dad had clients, not only in our town, but also throughout three counties. People wanted him to pave and/or seal their parking lots and driveways or lay down concrete. My dad would drive to the client and use a red pen for writing estimates. He did not use a calculator; he used his brain, for he was a math wiz. If he thought he was inaccurate, he would ask my brother Howard to review his calculations. It was rare that my dad was wrong. I admired how he handled his business. He was discrete and professional. He kept his finances in order and did not spend frivolously. We lived modestly. Did I mention that my dad did not graduate from high school? He was advanced academically, so he quit school. When he was growing up, they did not have assessments to measure your academic level. He knew as much as his teacher when it came to mathematics, so he stopped attending school.

When I was a child, I remember asking him to please explain his business and how it worked. He said, "No, go in the house," and called my mom to come and get me. I walked slowly into the house and while staring at him through the window, thought, *"One day I will show him."* I wanted that life style of working less than forty hours a week, being independent, and having a staff.

When he came home from working, he wanted us to keep the noise to a minimum. Tell that to a group of rambunctious children. We were loud as we played outside, riding bikes and scooters or jumping rope. We did anything that was noisy because we were kids. When one of us got out of hand or made too much noise outside, we had to come in and sit down. Well, we all ended up coming in, but we just brought the noise with us. My dad would tell us to be quiet and we would ignore him. He then asked my mom to keep us quiet so he could rest. We did for a while, but gradually, we would start making noise again. After awhile he would yell, "Be quiet, PLEASE!" We would laugh hysterically. I must confess that part of the joy we got from making that much noise was just to hear him say that. It was the only time he would show us his manners and we loved it. To this day we laugh and say to each other in our dad's voice, "Be quiet, PLEASE!"

About a week before my dad passed, I asked him to tell me about his business because I wanted my own, and he gave me this simple advice:

1. Know your business more than anyone else.
2. Never give a quote for less than the job is worth.

To substantiate that advice, he shared with me stories about some of his friends who had not followed those two simple rules. They ended up losing their businesses and going bankrupt. As the owner of two businesses, I often keep his advice in mind.

CHAPTER 7

Mr. Harvey Peek

That's my dad, Harvey Peek, at his birthday party.

My dad was a cool cat. When I share with others the joy of being part of a 15-member family, they are shocked and amazed. I remember in the second grade, I told my teacher that I had nine sisters and two brothers. She ignorantly asked if we were all by the same mother and father. I frowned at her and exclaimed, "Yes!" From that day on, I was reluctant to share my family dynamics. Today there is a reality show about a family of almost twenty children, so large families are becoming acceptable again.

My parents raised us to have good manners and be respectable. If we weren't, my dad would harp that we were showing bad manners and disrespect. So we were raised to work for what we wanted to get and not to cheat anyone or lie to people.

My father was old school when it came to grooming. He had a texturizer in his hair and kept it jet-black. He loved Sam Cook music and I often thought that's whom he was mimicking. He worked hard at his business and came home very dirty and sweaty. The tar from the asphalt got on his clothes and he had to shower and change clothes when he got home. But when it came to Sunday morning and going to church, he changed from that asphalt worker to Mr. Peek, with spit-shined shoes and a nice suit and tie. My dad loved to look good when going out. He kept his shoes shined and his suits dry cleaned. He attended the local Baptist church where he sang bass in the choir. My mom kept his shirts white as snow and pressed them on Saturday. It took my dad longer to get ready than my mom, and that amazed me!

My dad had a pick-up, a dump truck, a station wagon, and a Cadillac. His Cadillac was long and green with a white interior. That car was his pride and joy. He only drove it on special occasions, to church and funerals. The car's interior was white leather, and the car had power windows. He kept them locked so we couldn't play with the controls. It was rare that he let us drive it, even when we were old enough. We would sneak it out of the garage and put it back so he wouldn't realize that we had driven it. On my wedding day, he let me drive it and I ran over something in the road. I did not tell him. I saw no need to cause him stress.

One day at one of the churches in the neighborhood, my parents were asked to sing a Christmas song. Well, my sister and I dreaded that, because our parents never did that before, and we thought it would be awkward. When it came to singing, my dad was a pro. He took singing in the choir very seriously, and everything had to be perfect. My mom, on the other hand, took a more carefree approach; the Bible read make a joyful noise, and that is exactly what she did. She just sang.

Well, when it was time for them to perform, my dad started to clear his throat. While he was preparing, my mom just started singing. My sister and I fell out laughing. Singing bass, my dad wanted my mother to sing in harmony. Well, that wasn't gonna happen. She just blurted out in whatever key she felt comfortable singing, no matter how it came out. They were both sincere—just two different people. We laughed hysterically while watching them, because it was so comical to us.

CHAPTER 8

Mama Sees Angels

My mom told me this story when I was a child. It was her first encounter with angels. She told me not to be afraid, and I was fascinated and mesmerized. I mentally visualized the angels and hoped to see them one day like my mom did.

Mom said she was about eight or ten years old and was at the Baptist Church in Crawfordsville, Georgia. That was her family's church. This particular Sunday, as on every Sunday, the Pastor said if anyone wanted religion to come to the mourning bench and pray. "Wanting religion" would mean in today's language, deciding to accept Jesus as their Lord and Savior. After sitting nervously, Mama felt a tug in her heart to go forward. She slowly got up and quietly walked up to the front of the church. When her friends saw her, they joined her. She got to the mourning pew, kneeled down to pray, and with eyes closed, prayed to receive religion in her soul. She didn't notice anyone else around her as she kept praying. Suddenly, she had a vision of angels flying around her. She was so caught up in how the angels looked, that she was not afraid and just kept on praying. They wore white garments and had large wings. They were singing, "I love Jesus." She said they flew around her head, came to her ear singing, and flew away again. As they moved around her, tears began to stream down her face. She said she had never heard such beautiful sounding voices like that in all of her life. When she got up off her knees, she was afraid to shake the preacher's hand. When asked if she got religion, she shook her head yes.

She told her grandmother about seeing the angels and how beautifully they sang in her ear. Her grandmother replied that she was a special child because God showed her His angels. This story still fascinates me and gives me goose bumps because I can still picture the awe on my mom's face as she told this to me.

Her grandmother was right. My mom was a very special person who used her gift of discernment in worship and prayer. I say that when she saw the angels, one must have kissed her because she was such a sweet person.

CHAPTER 9

Bye, Mama, I'm Gonna Run Away

My childhood home

If there is ever a story I am known for in my family, it's my famous "running away" story, so here it goes...

Playing outside or watching TV was never a question for me. My father's favorite shows were the news and reruns of Hee-Haw and Lawrence Welk. The local news was on most of the time, so playing outside was a treat. We rode bikes and scooters, climbed trees and played hide-and-seek.

One day I did manage to persuade my dad to let us watch a movie. I don't remember the name of it. I just remember there was a girl in it around my age that was frustrated with her family and decided to run away. When her family discovered she was gone, they searched frantically until they found her, and everyone was happy. I wanted to do what I had seen that girl do on TV, so I decided to try it.

I picked a nice sunny day because I thought my family would appreciate the good weather when they came looking for me. I remember asking Mama repeatedly, "Can I run away now?" and she would ask what I was talking about. A few minutes later I would again ask her, "Mama, can I run away now?" After awhile she became weary of my nagging, and said, "Yes." I said, "Good, so bye Mama, I'll see you later–I'm leaving now." As I walked out of the driveway and up the dusty street, I got to the corner before Mama called, "Connäy (She always said my name in a southern way), come here." I ran back home and she spanked me, before saying, "Don't you ever run away again." I didn't have any idea of where I was going. I just wanted to be like that girl on TV. I wonder what mama thought of me asking to run away. She never brought it up again and for that I am thankful.

My brothers and sisters still laugh at this story, and say that I'm the only person who ever asked permission to run away.

CHAPTER 10

Think Yourself Happy

My mom was an outstanding teacher and preacher of the Gospel. The Lord placed her in many church roles from interim Pastor to Sunday School Teacher. Mama worked every aspect of ministry. She was Missionary President at the church, and loved mission work. Every second Sunday in the afternoon was Missionary Day.

As children, we were very influenced by Biblical Principles. I remember something called "Prayer Band," a group of women who went from house to house one day a week for Bible Study. When it was time for them to come to our house, Mama always made sure the house was clean and we were on our best behavior. The elderly women, who comprised the Prayer Band group, rarely smiled and always found Bible verses that scared me. They wore long, white dresses and thick opaque stockings. They were hard working, powerful women, and highly respected leaders in the church and community. My mom was the youngest of them, and I thought they wanted her to act old like them. I didn't want Mama to be around them, for they scared me. They sang old, slow songs and were always serious. My dad wasn't a fan of the Prayer Band ladies. He thought they took up too much of our time, and only allowed them to come over when he wasn't at home.

Prayer Band lady, Mother Haynes, with her husband, Elder Haynes

When they did come over, we had to sit very still and listen to them talk. I wanted to go outside and play, but Mama wouldn't let us during Prayer Band time. In their defense, I have to say that those ladies prayed many miracles in our family lives and others whom they touched.

My mom told me that she felt the call to preach and teach the Gospel, but for years, she was too scared to heed the call. When her younger children were in high school, Mama ventured out and began to preach and teach. She was a very logical and simplistic minister. She didn't have the Greek or Latin words, nor did she use the many different versions of the Bible. She only used the King James Version. She had much faith and tenacity. The word of God meant more to her than anything in the world and Mama was an avid Bible reader.

During one particular service when my mom preached, my dad, my siblings and I were in the audience. Mama preached from Acts 26:4, where Apostle Paul said, "I think myself happy." She gave an awesome sermon about that passage, and my dad told her he was very proud of her because she had preached so well. In fact, we all complimented her on that word. The sermon was about the power of the mind and how we can change our thoughts to influence our behavior.

I was happy to hear her and happy my dad was there to witness her ministering. To this day, many people still mention the message "Mother Peek" preached, called *Think*

Yourself Happy. I've had to remind myself several times to concentrate on good things and happiness would surely follow.

What story is most memorable about your loved one ?

Note from Dr. Constance

Did the memory make you laugh, smile or feel warm inside? If so, share that story to others keep their memory alive.

I Miss Talking to You

CHAPTER 11

Daddy to the Rescue

Me in grade school. I always wore dresses.

I don't consider myself a daddy's girl, because all ten of my dad's daughters were his pride and joy. My younger sister and I got away with more simply because we were the youngest. I like to think that the ten kids born before us wore them out so they gave in much easier with to us. Dad cared a lot for his daughters and would do anything within reason for us. He raised all of us to work hard and enjoy a great quality of life.

My mom was a devout Christian and dressed very modestly. She only wore dresses and skirts. Growing up, I never saw my mom in pants or pajamas. She raised us to be modest in our clothing, to stay wholesome, and always act like proper ladies. She thought that only men should wear pants, so she wouldn't let me wear them. When I finished grade school and was entering Junior high School, I wanted to wear pants. I spent all summer trying to convince Mama to change her mind, but she still refused. I had to wear dresses and I was unhappy wearing them. She allowed me to wear small high heels with my dresses and skirts, but still, no pants. She would say, "Pants are not ladylike and I want you to be ladylike."

It was time for school shopping and I was miserable, because I knew it would be skirts and dresses again. All of my friends wore pants. No one wore dresses as much as I did, and I was embarrassed. At the store, my mom purchased everything but pants, and I left the store with an attitude, although I couldn't let her know it.

When we got home I was discussing this with my mother. My father overheard us, and with one sentence, my life changed forever. He said, "Mamish," (my mom's name was Mamie but he always called her Mamish) "let her wear pants!" *Hallelujah*! My father had spoken, and I got to wear pants! No more answering questions from my friends about why I wore dresses all of the time. By the way, since I couldn't tell them the truth, my answers had often changed.

We went to the store before school started, and I got my first pair of blue jeans. Life was good. I wore them on the first day of school with pride.

I thought I was growing up, so when my mom asked me to do something, I started to sass her. Well, one time she was going to spank me, so I ran outside. She said that when I came back in the house she would spank me, but I said to myself, "*I won't go back in. Daddy helped me with the pants, and he will help me again.*" My dad wasn't home yet, but he was on his way. If I waited, he would let me in, and I wouldn't get a spanking. After waiting outside for about thirty minutes, I saw my dad driving down the street in his pickup truck. I was very happy and relieved. When he got out of the car, I ran to him and spoke softly. He asked me what I was doing outside. I told him mama was going to spank me. He told me to come inside with him, and when we walked in, you could have heard a pin drop. All eyes were on me. He said "Mamish, leave her alone." *Again, Daddy to the rescue*, I thought. My mom glared at me and said her famous line: "I will pay you for the old and the new." That was worse than any spanking I could have received. I thought about what just happened. I made up with Mama and learned a lesson, too. Never again would I use Daddy to get back at Mama.

Mom and dad, I really miss talking to you!

What are some of the favorite things your loved one did to make you feel special ?

Note from Dr. Constance:

I was a senior in high school and my mom bought me a sapphire ring like the other girls in my class. She used her reserved credit card to get it for me, because she knew it meant a lot to me. I smile every time I think of this act of kindness. When you think of what your love did to make you smile, now make someone else smile play it forward.

_____
_____
_____
_____
_____
_____
_____
_____

I Miss Talking to You

CHAPTER 12

Mama Cooks an Apple Pie

My mom cooking

I thought my mom was the best cook in the world. I loved it when she cooked my favorite dishes: homemade biscuits, rice pudding, teacakes (cookies), apple pie, and homemade candy. Sometimes before we left for school, she made us hot buttered biscuits and bacon and eggs. I would eat about three biscuits with syrup; it was the best!

I watched her cook, noticing she never relied on measuring utensils. She used her hand to measure the amount of an ingredient to add to the food she was preparing. I often admired how she could cook for a house full of people, yet still have food to feed others. If my father hadn't eaten yet, she would say, "I have to take some off for your father," so she would fix his plate and put it aside to keep us from eating it. Many times we would sneak and take some of his food because we liked it so much.

I had a toothache once when I was in the third grade. My parents took me to the dentist and I cried because it was so terrifying. The sound of the drill and the shot of Novocain caused me great anxiety. I dreaded going to the dentist.

Earlier in the day mama had baked an apple pie. I watched as she peeled the apples, made the crust, and added the ingredients. The smell of the pie baking was awesome. We all hung out in the kitchen until the pie was done. It came out of the oven hot, and she placed it on the stove to cool off. We all watched, wanting Mama to cut it so we could eat it. After it cooled down, we all got a slice of Mama's delicious pie. When I got my slice, I said, "Mama, it's not sweet enough, like your other pies." She said so lovingly, "You have a toothache, and I didn't want it to hurt any worse, so I did not put a lot of sugar in the pie." I said to myself, "Wow, Mama changed the recipe just for me!" So everyone had to eat apple pie that was not that sweet just because of me. I will never forget that story, and I share it often. The many sacrifices mama made for her family makes me grateful. She was truly the Proverb 31 woman.

As she got older, she cooked less and patronized country cooking restaurants in the area. I would ask her to make me some rice pudding or biscuits like she did when I was younger, but she would look at me with astonishment and say, "No, Mama don't cook like that anymore. I will buy it for you at the restaurant." I wasn't thrilled about that, I wanted Mama's cooking. Every now and then, though, she would call me on the phone and say, "Connäy, I made you some teacakes. Come and get them." I was there before she knew it, scarfing down Mama's food.

CHAPTER 13

Mama Goes To the Assisted Living Facility

I dread writing this part of the story because it still causes me great grief, sadness, and guilt. I must thank God for his comforting power and my family, friends, my church, and the hospice angels for their understanding.

After the first year of Mama's diagnosis, I started seeing signs of lapses in her memory. She asked me one day, "Connäy, do I have that forgetting disease?" I answered, "Yes, Mama." She said she thought so, and never asked me about it again. Then she became fixated on food. She would eat and still feel hungry, thinking that no one was feeding her. She asked me to buy her some food and I did, but after she ate it, she was hungry again within minutes.

During one stage of dementia, the patients get fixated on something like money or food and their metabolism increases greatly. You have to be careful not to take what they say to heart. I remember when my mom told me that I had a big "sit-a-pun," or rear end. I *had* gained a few pounds, but when Mama said it I felt so bad. One time she even thought I was pregnant. It hurt my feelings when Mama asked, "Connäy, are you pregnant again? Your stomach is getting big."

We kept my mom at home for as long as possible. Having dementia, Mom became very confused at times. She constantly asked where she was and said she wanted to go home. We would tell her that she was home and she would say ok, but five minutes later, she would ask again. We wrote her address on the dry erase board and had her read it to reiterate that she was home. That worked for a while, until she got frustrated and said, "I don't want to read that anymore." Home to a dementia patient may often be their childhood home, not their current residence. She would ask for her mother and ask when was her mother coming to get her. We would tell her that her mom was not here.

The hospice angels explained to me that my mom is not the mom I remember, but a new person that I am calling my mom. Mama never forgot who I was, however, nor who her God was. She would praise and pray all of the time. Her sleeping habits were off, and a few times she walked to a neighbor's home in the middle of the night. She would lose her balance while walking sometimes, so she was given a cane to assist her. She was a very proud and spry woman, so she would carry the cane like a stick, never using it to help her walk.

I was encouraged to use what Alzheimer's organizations call "therapeutic lying." You tell the patient that they cannot go home yet because the house is being cleaned or no one was there. You make up a reason they cannot go home. Being raised not to lie, I couldn't say such things.

With much counsel from the hospice angels, we agreed it was time to place Mom in an assisted living facility. That was the hardest thing I ever had to do in my life. We researched and visited a few facilities near her home, and decided on a place a few towns away. We chose a facility that was accustomed to working with dementia patients and knew their habits.

We transported her there, and she began to fit in. My mom talked in a loud voice and would tell everyone that Jesus was coming back soon. She would invite them to church and tell them they needed to be saved (smile).

The day we placed mom in the facility, I was looking at her and began to cry, tears pouring rapidly down my face. I felt I had disappointed her after all she did for me. When Mama saw me crying, she said, "Connäy, why are you crying? This is what happens when you get old. You be happy, look to Jesus, and hold your head up like Miss Ann. Mama is just old. And Connäy," she said, "Get yourself a house. The Lord will help you, so look to nobody but Him." I remember that conversation like it happened yesterday. I told mama that I would take care of her and told her not to worry. That was the last actual conversation I had with Mama. After that, she only spoke in one- and two-syllable words and smile a lot.

I visited Mom often (my brothers and sisters did also), and became a champion of Mama's care and new quality of life. I learned to how to read her face and understood what she could not tell me. I have to congratulate the assisted living facility staff for their patience with me. I was at first a thorn in their side, but it was my mom and I loved her. Thankfully, they began to understand my ways and me. When I would come to visit Mom, they would give me the answer to questions that I did not yet ask, but when my sister visited, they would hug her. I got the business treatment.

My brothers, sisters and I would visit mom at different times of the day to see how she was doing. One day she was staring at me and I knew something was wrong. I asked her what was wrong, but she did not answer and just kept looking at me. I prayed for the Lord to help me understand what was wrong with Mama. Immediately, it came to me she needed to use the bathroom. I got the nurse; she took mom to the bathroom, and yes, that is what she needed. When I visited Mama, I went into the bathroom with her and stayed in the bedroom while the nurses fed her. I checked her for sores, scratches and bruises, not necessarily because of negligence, but because of the disease and the behavior of the patient.

Visiting mom and seeing her in that condition, hurt me more than I can put into words. I questioned God and prayed for understanding. We would take mom outside in the wheelchair to enjoy the fresh air and sunshine, but she would say, "Now take me home, Connäy. Stop playing. I want to go home." She would yell to the attendants and nurses about taking her home and they would say, "Mamie you are home," and hug her. She knew her children and remembered our names when we went to see her, and that was very encouraging.

I kept my mom's words close to my heart. I aggressively looked for a house, and must have looked at almost fifty homes. On one visit to a home the realtor was giving me a tour. I went in one room and said, "I feel Mama. Mama is here with me, so this must be the right house." That was the first and only time I felt mama and felt her so strong. I did purchase the home. I shared with Mama when I visited, telling her that I got a home like she told me, and that I had felt her presence in the house. She looked at me, smiled, and opened her hands wide to hug me. She did not speak a word, but I knew she heard me and understood me. If she could have spoken, she would have said, "Connāy, I knew you would do it. You are a go-getter and the lead off."

How to Choose an Assisted Living Facility

Having to put a love one in an assisted living facility is not easy, it is very emotional. It can be one of the hardest decisions you have to make. From my experience I will share with you what I did and what worked and what did not. It may not be easy to see them in an Assisted Living Facility but know that they are getting the care they need.

1. **Tour Assisted Living Facilities** – I specifically went to the facilities that specialized in dementia patients.
    We toured several and chose the best that was best for our family.
2. **Talk to the Assisted Living Staff**
    I talked to the laundry personnel, cooks, aids, secretary and administrators. I wanted them to get to know me and my siblings. I wanted to know about how assisted living facilities function.
3. **Remember Assisted Living Facilities *assists* you in the care of your loved one**.
    Make sure you understand all decisions that are made; you must have input.
4. **Visit your loved one often.**

If you can't stay for 90 minutes stay for 30 minutes…just show up and care

5. **Look at the food menu of what your love one will be eating**

   Some facilities will allow you choose a meal for your love one. My mom loved biscuits so we made sure she had them with her meals.

6. **Choose a facility that you get to quickly if something should occur**

   We chose a facility that was pretty close to most of us.

CHAPTER 14

Mom Goes To Heaven

My mom transitioned on a Sunday morning that fell on St. Patrick's Day. It was one of the most painful moments of my life. Even if you know it's coming, you are never prepared for the death of a loved one. I would visit my mom frequently in the assisted living facility. I cannot say the word *Alzheimer,* nor the term *nursing home.* I have to use *dementia* to discuss what happened to my mom.

On one particular visit with mom I had come from a meeting and sat with her as she attempted to eat lunch. I talked to her and asked her how she was doing, but she just smiled at me and wouldn't speak. I wrestled with the thought of asking God to please stop her suffering. I wanted my mom back, the one that was sassy and wise. I missed her wit and laughter. I assisted her with lunch, and told her that I had to go back to the university to teach a class. She just smiled. I kissed her and prayed for her as I always did before going on my way.

About three hours later, I got a call from the hospice nurse telling me that Mom's condition had declined. I said, "No way, I was just there with her." She said Mama's temperature had dropped and they put her in the bed. She asked me to come by after work. I immediately went numb, and staring at my computer, said, "Help me, God." I went to see Mom, who was in the bed breathing quietly and slowly. The nurse said that Mom had a couple of days and told me to contact the family. Well, the family was contacted and came to see her. Mama smiled at each person talking to her.

Within forty-eight hours Mama's health had improved. I knew she wasn't 100% because I was not, and I felt like something was going to happen. I asked the hospice staff about Mom's sudden change. They explained that she might have come back because there was someone she wanted to see and/or someone needed to give an apology before a final goodbye. They went further to explain she might want to make sure everyone was okay before she left. I was heartsick and told my family and close friends what was said to me, so whoever needed to say their goodbye to Mom should do it. My mom was up in her chair, no longer in the bed, but I knew it wasn't for long.

After a couple of days and many visits from family and friends, my mom's health declined and she was back in the bed. During this time my brother and sister, Harvey and Ernestine, stayed overnight with her at the assisted living facility. On a Saturday afternoon, a hospice angel (I will call her that) came to visit my mom. She was the music therapist, and although she didn't work on Saturdays, it was pressed in her spirit to come visit my mom and sing moms favorite songs. She said she went online and did Google and YouTube searches for lyrics and music. She downloaded them and we sang Mom's favorite church songs to her. My brother took the lead on many of them, because I was too emotional. My mom lay there peacefully. Another hospice angel came to be with us through this final process. She relieved us so we could go home to get some rest, clean up, and eat.

Early Sunday morning, I called to check on mom. They said for me to come in and call the family again. Well, I did, and Mom was lying there as peacefully as if someone had rocked her to sleep. Hospice nurses explained to me how, during this final hour, Mom will transition when she wants to. We could be there or we could be absent, for it was up to her. I learned at that time the will of a person is powerful. All of us were at Mom's side, singing, crying, and rejoicing. We hugged each other and talked of the great times we had with Mama. The hospice angel explained to me again that mom would leave when she wanted, and for me not to be sad if she does when I am not around. I said I wanted to be there when she took her last breath.

I had stepped out to eat and gather my thoughts. It was at that time my mom chose to leave without me seeing her. The nurse explained to me that mom did not want me to see her leave. Mom didn't think I could take it. She was probably right. I shed a few tears and immediately shifted into watchdog mode over Mom's body. It was at that time I recalled that the human body was only a shell. The real part of our being is our soul, which goes back to God. The real person is not the shell or body in which it is housed.

CHAPTER 15

Homegoing Celebration "I Leave You Praise"

Preached by Bishop C. Shawn Tyson

My good friend and sister in Christ, Evangelist Sherri Brogdon helped me to process this unwelcome thing called "death." As my family prepared for her Homegoing service, I had to get a picture of mom for the obituary, and assist my family with the burial arrangements. My sister Debbie wrote the obituary, God bless her. She took the initiative and wrote it. I called Sherri Brogdon and said that there were many things on my mind about my mom's transition, but I knew Mama would want me to get my hair done. She always encouraged us to look our best. I just blurted out to Evangelist Sherri, "I need to get my hair done, but I cancelled two appointments already." She gently said go get your hair done. It was as if Mama was saying, "It's okay, get your hair done." For her burial, my sister Ernestine bought Mom a beautiful white outfit and I had a white blouse of Mom's that went with it. My sister

Bridie gave to Debbie Mom's favorite scripture, John 14:1-3, to be added to the obituary. My brothers Harvey and Howard were the Rock of Gibraltar.

A Homegoing Service is a celebration of the life and legacy of the person that transitioned to Heaven. The day of my mom's Homegoing Service was a snowy day, March 22nd. From the day of Moms transition to her Homegoing service, the weather had abruptly changed. I like to believe greatness had left the earth and the weather responded accordingly.

Our Pastor, Bishop C. Shawn Tyson, preached the service like no other. His title was "I Leave You Praise." He shared with us how God had told him early in the morning that He would bless the Peek legacy and we will go from great, to greater, to greatest in God. He also said that Mom left us the legacy of her praise and love for God. First Lady Krista Tyson sang Mom's favorite songs. The church was filled with dignitaries, community leaders, and friends.

The Spirit of the Lord filled the Sanctuary. I remember dancing in the spirit, and my brother Howard dancing in the aisle. All of Mom's children were giving God praise for her life and legacy.

This was truly a Homegoing celebration.

My sisters and I (left to right), Velma, Dr. Betty and Ernestine.

CHAPTER 16

Christmastime at the Peek's Home

Of all of the holidays, Christmas is my favorite. I love the happiness and joyful feeling that seems to take over me. Growing up in a small rural area, in a state in the midwestern part of the United States, the snow seemed to start in November and leave in early April. Preparing for the winter was a way of life for us. We heated the house with coal and coal oil. The house would be warm in the daytime and the temperature would go down at night. I would hear my mom start a fire with coal and turn on the furnace early in the morning so it would be warm when the rest of us got up.

I began to ask my parents for Christmas gifts early. I wanted Barbie Dolls, Easy Bake Oven, and board games. I would watch the toy commercials and I would go berserk. I would scream, "Mama can I have it, will you get it for me?" or, if my father was near I would ask him for what I wanted and get the famous answer, "We'll see." I hated that line because it meant if he had to think about it, I might not get the toy.

But on Christmas Day, we managed to have toys and gifts. I don't remember having a Christmas tree, but I'm sure we did. I was more concerned about the toys. One thing for sure, my father would always have for us a Christmas bag. I think this was one of his childhood traditions that he passed on to us. We so looked forward to getting that Christmas bag. It consisted of an apple, orange, Christmas candy, and nuts. I remember appreciating that Christmas bag as much as I appreciated the Christmas gifts. My father would celebrate and say, "This is the first Christmas Day." I never understood what that meant. I bet it was another southern saying that I grew accustomed to hearing.

At church we had a Christmas program where we all had to say a speech that we learned in front of the church. My brother Howard and I sang a song, "When the Gates Swing Wide," an old song about entering into the pearly gates. Howard wasn't a fan of singing with me and was made to do it almost every Christmas. I took the lead and he stood there pretending to sing. I must say now I don't blame Howard. It was a slow song, and we were only ten

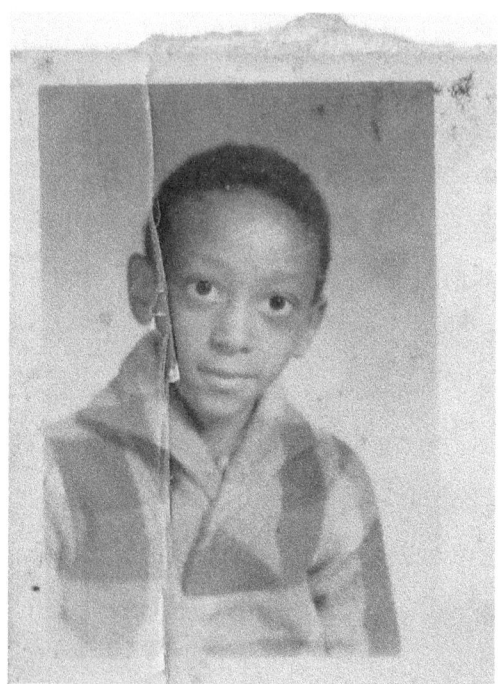

My brother Howard in grade school

and eight years old, much too young to be singing about entering in the Pearly Gates. Next, each child who attended that church would get up and say the speech that they had memorized. I would stand up with glee and say my speech; it was scary at first, but then I did it. That could have been the beginning of my speaking career. After the church program we would form a line, from the youngest to the oldest, and each was handed (You can guess), another brown bag of candy, fruit, and a box of raisins. I liked when we formed such a line because I was always at the beginning. The brown lunch bag had a red or green ribbon tied around it and they were in a laundry basket. We walked slowly forward, took our bag, and went to our seats.

Christmas time meant a two-week break from school. It was mayhem on my parents, trying to keep us occupied. We played outside a lot, making snow angels and snowmen. We played indoors with the toys we received until we got bored with them, and back outside we went. We had a pile of coal that we used for heat, and when covered by the snow, it looked like a mountain. We would run on it and declare that we were "King of the Mountain" until someone would push us off and gain the title. I think about it now, and wonder what kept us from falling and getting seriously injured on the slippery, wet, snow-covered pile of coal. God had his angels watching over us. We couldn't have a lot of friends coming over. My parents thought there were enough of us without adding more kids in the yard. When we did have company, it was fun and chaotic. We shared our toys and games and enjoyed the innocence of our childhood.

To this day, at Christmastime I have fruit, candy, raisins and nuts for my family. The appreciation for it is not as grand as I would like, but I still have it anyway. It was a part of my childhood. The "First Christmas Day," as my dad would say, is still my favorite holiday. During the holiday time, embrace the memory of your loved ones and hug the ones that are dear to you.

CHAPTER 17

We are Family

I have to compliment the Peek crew. We are a God-fearing, business-minded, and intelligent family. We hold Bachelor, Master, or Doctorate degrees. In our family are business owners, marketing specialists, preachers/evangelist, deacons, a college professor, and Pastor (Dr. Betty Peek-March). I often stare at my family when we are together, and listen to the various conversations going on around me. Some talk about the world crisis, the political climate, or strategic planning and marketing. Since my career is in higher education, I bore the rest of them with educational matters and the importance of getting a college degree. The whole gathering turns into a buffet of critical thinkers engaging in conversation. We are mild-mannered and forgiving to a fault, extending to people what we call "P.C." (Peek Charm). All twelve of us love to smile, and I often tease my younger sister Lisa about how we are "The Smilin' Peeks." Whether we are happy, sad, or mad, we are sure to smile.

When I was growing up, my brother Howard worked a lot with our dad in the asphalt business. Dad was grooming Howard to take over the family business. My brother is a math wiz like Dad, and a very articulate and confident person. Howard and I often banter back and forth about frivolous things, just to see what makes sense and what doesn't. But underneath it all, we still try to match wits with each other. I give in most of the time, because my brother becomes relentless in challenging me.

After working with dad, when Howard got paid, it was a fun time for Lisa and me. He would buy candy, McDonalds food, comic books, and soda. We would beg him to get us something that he wouldn't, and then tell Daddy, who made Howard share with us. Even though he didn't always share candy or other treats willingly, when Howard got paid, we went to the Laundromat and he would pay to have our clothes and blankets washed. Yes, we had a washer at home, but only one washer for a house full of kids made it too time consuming. On Howard's payday, I would have my clothes all in the basket ready to go, and we went after he had eaten. One summer he bought food for all of us to go on a picnic. I know he doesn't think I remember, but I do. We wanted to go on a picnic, so we went to the local grocery store, put all this food in the basket, and Howard paid for it. So now, when he begins to annoy me, I remember how he helped Lisa and me while we were growing up. Then I rescind my arguments and let him win.

CHAPTER 18

Conclusion Of The Matter

I could go on with many beautiful memories about my parents. The pain that is felt when a loved one transitions can be unbearable. But there is hope for those of you going through the same experience. When my parents went to Heaven, I knew it would be hard. But no one told me *how* hard was hard, or just how difficult it would become before I knew to seek help from a grief counselor.

No one could tell me because I had to experience it for myself. When my mom passed, for months I still picked up the phone, intending to dial the assisted living facility in order to check on her. I had to keep reminding myself, *she's not there*.

When my dad passed, for weeks I kept looking for him to come into the driveway with his green pickup truck. I couldn't stop looking out the window for him. After a few weeks, I accepted the fact that he wasn't going to, and I had to deal with it.

I had to learn that the world does not stop because Dr. Constance Peek Longmire is experiencing grief and is missing her mother. The world keeps going and a person must go on too. I remember one day my niece Mimi called to check on me, and I told her how I hated the world, because it wouldn't stop. I just wanted the world to stop and everyone be still. She said, "Auntie, you can't hate the world, it will be alright." That simple line snapped me out of it and continues to snap me out of it.

I have to live for my family but for mostly for myself. That is what my parents would want me to do. After my mom passed, I told my beautiful children how unfair it is for them to have a mother but I do not. I stressed how it was unjust to me. They listened attentively and commented with their silence. I stared at them and then walked away. I now know that it was grief speaking because I was hurt.

If you are going through a similar situation, you will need a strong support system to help you understand what you are experiencing and help you get through it. Do not get stuck in pain or sorrow. My Pastor, Bishop Shawn Tyson, encouraged me to still talk to my mom even though she is in Heaven. He stressed how good and healthy it is to keep her memory alive in my mind. First Lady Tyson told me one day, "Dr. Longmire, you have your mother's ways." Oh, sweet Jesus, how that helped me. I knew I had her thin lips and pointy nose, but to realize I also have her love of God and love for people is amazing to me. Along with her administrative skills, I also have my dad's business savvy.

We would visit mom consistently, my sister Pastor Dr. Betty (a recent widow) would come to visit mom and sing and pray for her. A gentlemen (Mr. Tom) from my church (a widower) would come to visit my mom also. Noting his love and care for our mom, my sister Ernestine and I decided to introduce him to Betty. Well they met and have been inseparable since. They recently married. I think that is very cool, they both met while caring for mom. So somehow mama set them up.

Thank you to the Hospice Angels:

Mary N, Jane, Desirrae, Sheila, Shonita, Kathy and the those whose name we did not mention. I thank you all from the bottom of my heart.

Thank you to the Assistant Living Facility Dementia Ward staff, laundry aids, nurses, doctors, secretarial staff and nurses assistants…..we couldn't have completed this journey without you all. Thank you for caring for my mom Mrs. Mamie Peek.

How to Care for a Caregiver

If you are a caregiver, may I suggest that you do the following:

- Rest
- Take care of yourself
- Exercise
- Make a date with yourself do something positive for YOU
- Talk to someone (a Spiritual Counselor, Grief Counselor)
- Seek a dependable support system
- Complete the Caregiver's Self Management Map that I created on pages 79-82.

Notes:

I Miss Talking to You

Constance J. Longmire Ph.D

Biography

Constance J. Longmire is an Instructor at a renown research university. She attended Akron University and received her Doctorate Degree from Seminary.

She has been evaluated as an outstanding instructor and analytic problem solver. She serves as a member of NOCHE and OACAC, NEOEA and she is Quality Matters Certified to teach online classes.

Dr. Longmire received the President's Excellence Award which honors those who are making a difference on campus. She is a graduate of President Lefton's "Leadership for Excellence," a 10-month extensive and accelerated leadership program. Her campus received the "2012 Trail Blazer Award" for her outstanding work in the area of Diversity and Community Involvement.

Her love for students and adult learning fueled the passion for her own business where she worked closely with school districts and their administration. She continues to host several adult learning seminars and presentations.

She has served on several panels for educational reform, such as the Educational Panel for the Cleveland Metropolitan School District with Mr. Bill Cosby (the entertainer) and Dr. Bernice King (daughter of Dr. Martin Luther King).

After the passing of her mom to dementia, she wrote "I Miss Talking to You," a book designed to help and encourage caregivers.

She is a requested speaker, author, preacher of the Gospel and educator. For all speaking engagements, you may contact her at email address:

longmireconstance@yahoo.com.

Dr. Longmire is married to Kenneth Longmire and they have two children, K. Matthew and Kaylyn.

Dr. Constance Peek Longmire's
SELF MANAGEMENT M.A.P.

Motivational Application Process

Part I

designed this M.A.P. (Motivational Application Process) to help all caregivers take care of themselves.

Please complete the following questions and review them daily. A map is an instructional document that will get you from one point to another. This M.A.P. will encourage you to keep moving and not get stuck in sadness or despair. You will grow in emotional stamina and fortitude and have a smile that is genuine.

You must always have something to look forward to or to keep your eyes on the prize.

List your GOALS:

1. _____
2. _____
3. _____
4. _____
5. _____

Daily Confessions

1. I am smart
2. I am kind and good
3. I am loved
4. I am forgiven
5. _____
6. _____
7. _____

When I am sad I will…

1. Walk
2. Pray/meditate
3. Call someone
4. Count my blessings
5. _____
6. _____
7. _____
8. _____
9. _____
10. _____

Dr. Constance Peek Longmire's
SELF MANAGEMENT M.A.P.

Motivational Application Process

Part II

As a caregiver you must remain healthy not only for the person(s) you are caring for but more importantly for yourself. You must take care yourself mentally or physically.

Please avail yourself to resources and agencies that will assist you.

My Support System

1. *Dr. Constance Peek Longmire*
2. *Social Services*
3. _____
4. _____
5. _____
6. _____
7. _____

I will take daily care of myself by...

1. Drinking water
2. Exercising weekly
3. Have ME time
4. Laugh more

5. _____
6. _____
7. _____

I Miss Talking to You

www.ingramcontent.com/pod-product-compliance
Lightning Source LLC
Chambersburg PA
CBHW071227160426
43196CB00012B/2432